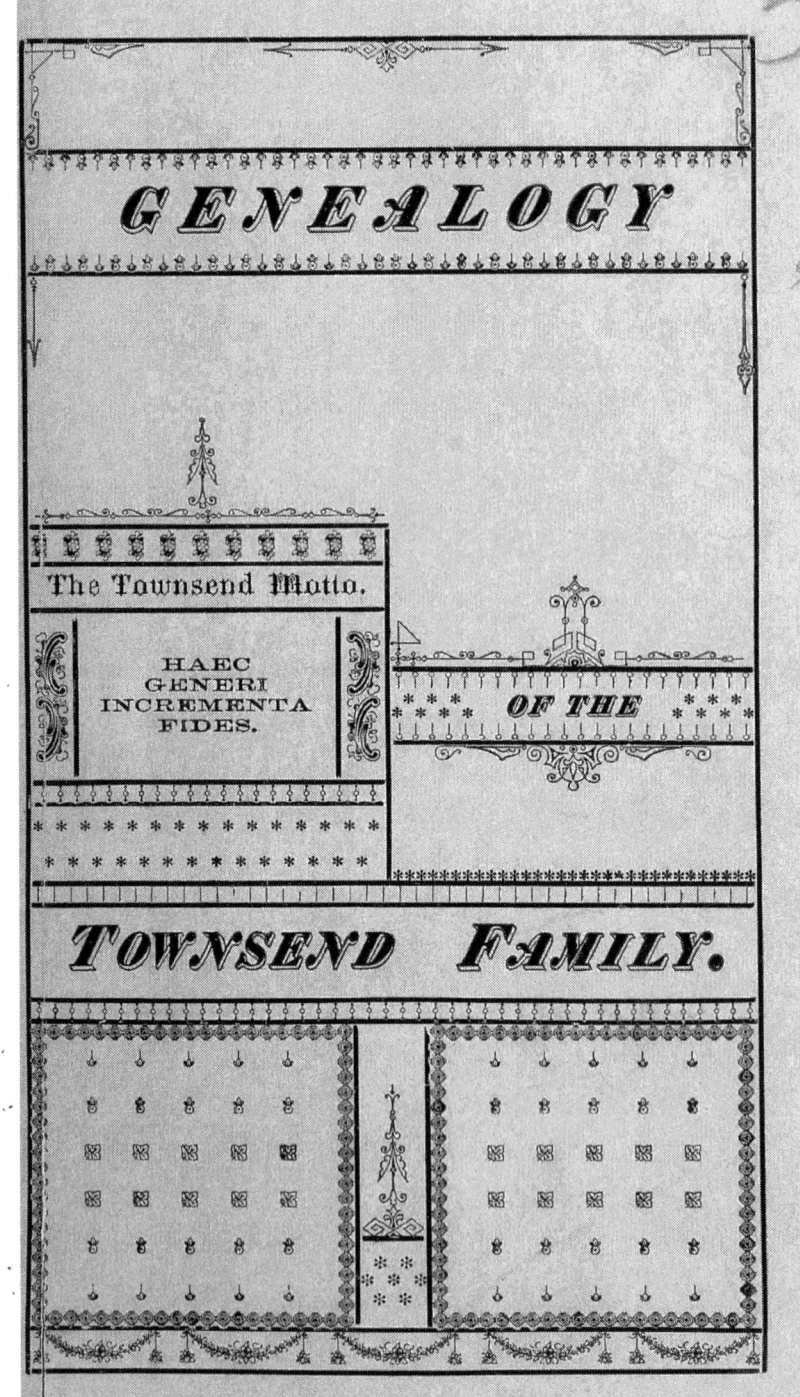

GENEALOGY

OF THE

TOWNSEND FAMILY.

COMPILED BY

BENJAMIN D. TOWNSEND,

OF LIME SPRING, IOWA.

ALFRED CENTRE, N. Y.:
THE AMERICAN SABBATH TRACT SOCIETY'S STEAM PRINT.
1879.

England. Walter Atte Townshende, son of Sir Lodovic de Townshende, a Norman nobleman, whom Collins, in his Peerage of England, puts at the head of this family, flourished soon after the Conquest. This Lodovic, it seems, married Elizabeth de Hauteville, sole heir of Raynham, daughter of Sir Thomas de Hauteville, of the famous family of de Hauteville, or Haville, which family at this time appears to have been a most important one. They were of Norman extraction, and, settling in the county of Norfolk, became possessed of a considerable property, said to have been granted them by William the Conqueror, which, by marriage, came to the Townsend family. We find the name in ancient deeds written thus: Ad-Finem-Ville, Ad-Exitum-Ville. William Ad-Exitum-Ville, that is, Townsend or Tunneshende, held considerable lands of the prior of Norwiche's lordship in Taverham, Norfolk, in the reign of King John, A. D. 1200."

Trusting that the lost link in the Townsend genealogy will soon be restored, and in the hope that this little work may more fully unite so numerous a people as the Townsends are, it is now submitted to my kindred.

BENJAMIN D. TOWNSEND.

Lime Spring, Iowa, February, 1879.

GENEALOGY

– OF –

JONATHAN TOWNSEND.

JONATHAN TOWNSEND (my great-grandfather)
MARRIED
HULDAH NEWTON.

They had seven children: Jonathan, Jr., born January 21st, 1766; Martin, born ——, died young; Sally, born ——, died, being a young woman; Benjamin, born about 1769; Nancy, born January 17th, 1771; Polly, born June 17th, 1772; Eliphalet, born February 2d, 1775. All seven children were born in New Salem, Franklin Co., Massachusetts. Jonathan Townsend, Sr., died when Eliphalet, the youngest child, was about one year of age. His widow was soon married to Daniel Curtis, by whom she had one child, a daughter, and died in the winter of 1813. Their oldest son, Jonathan, Jr., married Mary Haskell for his first wife, by whom he had two children, when she died. For his second wife he married Olive Phiney, who was born September 20th, 1769.

Names of their Children.

1. SALLY TOWNSEND, born June 1st, 1785; died in Waseca county, Minnesota, June 24th, 1869.
2. JONATHAN, Jr., 2d, born May 15th, 1787; died in 1858.
3. UZIAL, born November 2d, 1790; died August 13th, 1864.
4. SUEL, born January 27th, 1793; died September 29th, 1827.
5. OLIVE, born July 7th, 1795; died January 2d, 1826.
6. HULDAH, born December 15th, 1797; lived in Franklin county, Iowa, July, 1878.

NOTE.—Jonathan, Jr., 2d, Suel, Olive, Noah, and Adin died in Concord, Erie Co., N. Y. Uzial died in Illinois, seventeen miles west of Chicago. Their father, Jonathan, Jr., died in the town of Collins, Erie Co., N. Y., October 21st, 1838. His widow, Olive Phiney, died in Concord June 4th, 1862.

7. NOAH, born February 13th, 1801; died February 14th, 1853.
8. ELVIRA, born August 30th, 1803; alive July, 1878.
9. HOSEA WILLIAM, born March 30th, 1807; alive 1878.
10. DIADAMA, born May 13th, 1810.*
11. ADIN, the youngest, was born in Concord, Erie Co., N. Y., August 10th, 1813; died 1844.

Separate Families of Jonathan Townsend, Jr.

EPHRAIM ALLEN BRIGGS† (No. 12)
MARRIED
SALLY TOWNSEND (No. 1).

They had eleven children, and were as follows:
13. MARY ELVIRA BRIGGS, born May 9th, 1808.
14. EPHRAIM T. BRIGGS, born June 8th, 1810.
15. SYLVIA BRIGGS, born August 5th, 1811.
16. THOMAS M. BRIGGS, born March 23d, 1813.
17. JONATHAN BRIGGS, born February 12th, 1815.‡
18. ERASMUS BRIGGS, born August 31st, 1818.
19. SUEL BRIGGS, born April 17th, 1820.
20. SALLY BRIGGS, born March 17th, 1823.
21. CINDERRILLA BRIGGS, born October 5th, 1825.
22. CHRISTOPHER BRIGGS, born March 21st, 1828.
23. CHANDLER C. BRIGGS, born July 20th, 1830.

MARY E. BRIGGS (No. 13)
MARRIED
WILLIAM FIELD (No. 24).

Their children were,
25. MARVIN W. FIELD.
26. MARY LOVINA FIELD.
27. CHARLES FIELD.
28. EMILY FIELD.
29. PERRY FIELD, died in 1864.
30. SALLY FIELD.
31. MANLEY FIELD.

---

* The first ten children of Jonathan Townsend, Jr., were all born in New Salem, Franklin Co., Massachusetts. In 1811, Jonathan and his wife Olive removed to Concord, Erie Co., N. Y.

† Ephraim Allen Briggs, born March 10th, 1783; died February 25th, 1861.

‡ The above five were all born in Orange, Franklin Co., Massachusetts; removed to Concord, Erie Co., N. Y., in 1815, where all the rest of the children were born.

EPHRAIM T. BRIGGS (No. 14)
MARRIED
JANE FLEMMINGS (No. 32).

Their children were,
33. JANE ANN BRIGGS, died July 16th, 1865.
34. GEORGE W. BRIGGS, died 1843.
35. MARIA BRIGGS, died January 31st, 1865.
36. VIOLA BRIGGS.

SYLVIA BRIGGS (No. 15)
MARRIED
STANY KING (No. 37).

Their children were,
38. ALLEN KING, died in 1855.
39. DIANTHA KING.
40. DIANA KING.

THOMAS M. BRIGGS (No. 16)
MARRIED
PHŒBE SPAULDING (No. 41).

Their children were,
42. ALLEN BRIGGS.
43. GEORGE W. BRIGGS.
44. DELIA BRIGGS.
45. MANIS BRIGGS.
46. JENNIE BRIGGS.
47. FAYETTE BRIGGS, died in 1869.
48. CHANCY BRIGGS.

Jonathan (No 17) and Erasmus (No. 18) not married in 1877.

SUEL BRIGGS (No. 19)
MARRIED
PHŒBE BALLOU (No. 49).

They had no children.

SALLY BRIGGS (No. 20)
MARRIED
ORVIL S. CANFIELD (No. 50).

Their children were,
51. CHARLES CANFIELD.
52. NEWMAN CANFIELD.
53. LAURA CANFIELD.
54. ORVIL CANFIELD.

CINDERRILLA BRIGGS (No. 21)
MARRIED
WILLIAM SMITH (No. 55).

Their children were,
56. ALPHONSO SMITH.
57. ANGERONA SMITH.
58. CHARLES E. SMITH.
59. LORAINE SMITH.
60. LOVETTE SMITH, died in 1875.
61. ELLA SMITH.
62. LUZERNE SMITH.
63. MARY A. SMITH.
64. WILLIAM D. SMITH.
65. LILLIE O. SMITH.
66. ALLEN L. SMITH.

CHRISTOPHER BRIGGS (No. 22)
MARRIED
JANE COLBURN (No. 67).

They had one child,
68. CHARLOTTE M. BRIGGS.

CHANDLER C. BRIGGS (No. 23)
MARRIED
PHŒBE JANE WOODWARD (No. 69).

Their children were,
70. AUTHER BRIGGS.
71. SUEL C. BRIGGS.

NOTE.—Mary Elvira Briggs Field died in March, 1847; Ephraim T. Briggs died June 30th, 1848; Cinderrilla Briggs Smith died July 5th, 1874. Thomas M. Briggs and Suel Briggs live in LaCrosse county, Wisconsin, 1877; Jonathan Briggs lives in Garnavillo, Clayton Co., Iowa: Sally Briggs Canfield lives in Freedom, Waseca Co., Minnesota; Chandler C. Briggs lives at Blue Earth City, Minnesota.

JONATHAN TOWNSEND, Jr., 2d, (No. 2)
MARRIED
BETSEY DAVIS (No. 72).

They had no children. He died in 1858.

UZIAL TOWNSEND (No. 3)*
MARRIED
PATTY WHEELER (No. 73).

They had one son,
74. GILBERT W. TOWNSEND, born February 12th, 1812.

SUEL TOWNSEND (No. 4)†
MARRIED
POLLY WHEELER (No. 75).

They had two children,
76. LYSANDER TOWNSEND.
77. WHEELER TOWNSEND.‡

OLIVE TOWNSEND (No. 5)§
MARRIED
KENDALL JOHNSON (No. 78).

They had five children,
79. KENDALL JOHNSON.
80. SARAH JOHNSON.
81. DAVID JOHNSON.
82. CHARLES JOHNSON.
83. RUTH JOHNSON.

HULDAH TOWNSEND (No. 6)
MARRIED
ENOCH ST. CLAIR (No. 84).‖

---

* Uzial died August 13th, 1864; his wife died March 17th, 1846.
† Suel died September 29th, 1827.
‡ They live in the north part of Grant county, Wisconsin, 1877.
§ Olive died January 2d, 1826.
‖ They were married at Concord, Erie Co., N. Y., December 9th, 1816, by Amaziah Ashman, Esq. Enoch was born September 1st, 1790, and died at his residence near Hampton, Franklin Co., Iowa, April 3d, 1873.

They had ten children,

85. ROXALENA, born November 1st, 1818, and died August 13th, 1822.
86. LOUISA L., born April 10th, 1821, married
87. RALPH BENNETT November 22d, 1847.
88. ELISABETH S., born July 24th, 1823, married
89. PETER M. HOFFMAN February 14th, 1855.
90. BENJAMIN, born April 26th, 1825, died July 26th, 1825.
91. Son, born January 29th, 1829, died February 3d, 1829.
92. LOIS JOSEPHINE, born July 18th, 1830, married
93. LEWIS MILTON STEVENSON November 4th, 1849.

[They had two children: 94. FLORELL F. STEVENSON, born October 1st, 1850. 95. ADELL A. STEVENSON, born February 13th, 1855.]

96. R. CLEMENTINE, born June 25th, 1833, married
97. CHARLES J. TOBEY December 28th, 1860.
98. LAURA E., born May 22d, 1835.
99. MARY J., born April 28th, 1837, married
100. THOMAS W. JONES April 6th, 1864.
101. AUGUSTINE D. ST. CLAIR, the tenth and last child, born July 31st, 1839, married
102. FLORENCE J. JAKEWAY January 28th, 1872. She was born April 7th, 1851.

[They had three children: 103. WINNIE CELIA ST. CLAIR, born January 22d, 1873. 104. EDSON DEWITT ST. CLAIR, born October 26th, 1874. 105. FRANK EARLE ST. CLAIR, born November 22d, 1876. Residence, Reeve Township, Franklin Co., Iowa.]

NOAH TOWNSEND (No. 7)*

MARRIED

ACHSAH WHEELER (No. 106).

They had six children,
107. PARMELIA TOWNSEND.
108. SANFORD TOWNSEND.
109. SALLY TOWNSEND.
110. ALMEDA TOWNSEND.
111. HARRISON TOWNSEND.
112. LOUISA TOWNSEND.

[All living in 1877; residence not given.]

---

*Noah died February 14th, 1853.

ELVIRA TOWNSEND (No. 8)
MARRIED
WILLIAM F. OWEN (No. 113).*

They had one child,

114. WILLIAM P. OWEN, born at Concord, Erie Co., N. Y., October 22d, 1823.

WILLIAM P. OWEN (No. 114)
MARRIED
HULDANA S. BOOTHE (No. 115).†

They had three children,
116. IRENE M. OWEN.
117. LILLIE I. OWEN.
118. ALSON WILLIAM OWEN. Farmers at Spring, Crawford Co., Pa., in 1878.

HOSEA WILLIAM TOWNSEND (No. 9)
MARRIED
MARGARETTA RUDEN (No. 119).‡

They had seven children,
120. MARGARETTA ELLEN, born February 15th, 1831.
121. GEORGE WASHINGTON, born January 29th, 1833.
122. RICHARD ALLEN, born April 30th, 1835.
123. MARY, born April 11th, 1837.
124. SARAH, born April 20th, 1839.
125. EDWARD BENNET, born April 10th, 1846.
126. S. MILES S., born June 10th, 1849; died September 9th, 1853.

H. W. Townsend's Children's Marriages, and their Families.

M. ELLEN TOWNSEND (No. 120)
MARRIED
HIRAM T. GREEN (No. 127).§

---

* They were married December 6th, 1821, and he died June 28th, 1867.

† They were married April 26th, 1847; she was from Spring, Pa.

‡ They were married in Buffalo, N. Y., December 20th, 1829. She was born in Lockport, N. Y., October 15th, 1813.

§ They were married November 2d, 1859, by Rev. J. Hazard Hartzell, a Universalist minister. Hiram was born May 25th, 1828. They reside in their own house, No. 75 Seventh Street, Buffalo, N. Y.

NOTE.—Edward B. Townsend was born in Lafayette, Indiana, and S. Miles S. Townsend was born at Oak Orchard, Orleans Co., N. Y.; all the other five were born in Buffalo, N. Y. H. W. Townsend's place of residence, June 19th, 1878, was No. 69 Seventh Street, Buffalo.

They had one child,

128. GEORGE TOWNSEND GREEN, born February 13th, 1866; died December 27th, 1869.

GEORGE WASHINGTON TOWNSEND (No. 121)
MARRIED
HATTIE A. AUSTIN (No. 129).*

They never had any children.

RICHARD A. TOWNSEND (No. 122)
MARRIED
MARY M. ADAMS (No. 130).†

They had four children,

131. ALLEN MILES, born November 6th, 1861.
132. IDA ADAMS, born May 3d, 1866.
133. HARRIET MARGERETTA, born July 8th, 1868.
134. FRANK EDWARD, born March 6th, 1874; died July 30th, 1874.

MARY TOWNSEND (No. 123)
MARRIED
GEORGE S. WARDWELL (No. 135).‡

They had six children,

136. GEORGE TOWNSEND WARDWELL, born August 28th, 1864.
137. MARY MARGARETTA WARDWELL, born May 5th, 1866.
138. FRANK CHANDLER WARDWELL, born June 10th, 1868.
139. WILLIAM HENRY WARDWELL, born June 8th, 1872.
140. CHARLES U. WARDWELL, born July 1st, 1874.
141. EDWARD TOWNSEND WARDWELL, born August 12th, 1876.

---

*They were married October 31st, 1861, by Rev. J. Hazard Hartzell. Hattie was born August 23d, 1839. They reside in their own house, No. 351 Pearl Street, Buffalo, N. Y.

†They were married December 19th, 1860, by the same minister. Mary was born February 1st, 1839. June 19th, 1878, they resided in a house they erected some years ago, No. 47 Seventh Street, Buffalo, N. Y.

‡They were married June 9th, 1863, by the same minister. George was born August 29th, 1829. They now (June 19th, 1878) reside in their own house, No. 235 Hudson Street, Buffalo, N. Y.

SARAH TOWNSEND (No. 124)
MARRIED
FRANK M. CHANDLER (No. 142).*

They had five children,

143. FRANK TOWNSEND CHANDLER, born June 30th, 1864; died June 30th, 1864.
144. GRACE HARRIET CHANDLER, born November 18th, 1865; died February 10th, 1868.
145. MARTHA ELLEN CHANDLER, born July 14th, 1868.
146. MARGARET CHANDLER, born April 7th, 1870.
147. SARAH BELL CHANDLER, born September 25th, 1873.

EDWARD B. TOWNSEND (No. 125)
MARRIED
ANNA P. COURTER (No. 148).†

They had four children,

149 ANNA COURTER, born May 14th, 1869; died November 3d, 1874.
150. SARAH LOUESE, born August 20th, 1872.
151. FLORENCE MAY, born January 17th, 1875.
152. HIRAM EDWARD, born June 27th, 1877; died April 4th, 1878.

DIADAMA TOWNSEND (No. 10)
MARRIED
ALANSON WHEELER (No. 153).‡

They had two children,

154. DAVID WHEELER.
155. CHARLES WHEELER.

ADIN TOWNSEND (No. 11)§
MARRIED
ELECTA MITCHELL (No. 156).

---

*They were married August 13th, 1861, by Rev. J. Hazard Hartzell. Frank was born March 30th, 1835. They reside (June 19th, 1878) at Titusville, Pennsylvania.

† They were married May 21st, 1868, by Rev. O. Witherspoon, an Episcopal minister. Anna was born May 17th, 1843. June 19th, 1878, they resided in their own house, No. 72 Seventh Street, Buffalo, N. Y.

‡ They live in Concord, Erie Co., N. Y.

§ Adin died in 1844.

They had several children, *
157. OLIVE TOWNSEND.
158. CHARLES TOWNSEND.
159. JOHN TOWNSEND. They live West.

Gilbert W. Townsend's Family Record.

GILBERT W. TOWNSEND (No. 74)
MARRIED
ESTHER TWITCHEL (No. 160).†

They had eleven children,
161. MARY TOWNSEND, born February 25th, 1829.
162. DULCENIA TOWNSEND, born August 7th, 1830.
163. ALBERT U. TOWNSEND, born April 29th, 1832.
164. LYSANDER TOWNSEND, born January 13th, 1834.
165. PERRY S. TOWNSEND, born December 21st, 1835.
166. CHARLES D. TOWNSEND, born January 15th, 1838.
167. GEORGE S. TOWNSEND, born November 20th, 1840.
168. AUGUSTUS TOWNSEND, born December 4th, 1842.
169. CYRUS E. TOWNSEND, born January 7th, 1845.
170. ELIZA TOWNSEND, born March 10th, 1847.
171. MARTHA TOWNSEND, born December 27th, 1848.

Their Marriages.

161. MARY TOWNSEND married (172) CHESTER PLUMMER September 17th, 1848.
162. DULCENIA TOWNSEND married (173) CHARLES DUEL December 23d, 1851.
163. ALBERT U. TOWNSEND married (174) ELIZABETH WHITMORE January 18th, 1852.
164. LYSANDER TOWNSEND died March 8th, 1864.
165. PERRY S. TOWNSEND married (175) ANGELINE WEABER December 7th, 1865.
166. CHARLES D. TOWNSEND married (176) LAZELLEE ELDRIDGE March 1st, 1859.
167. GEORGE S. TOWNSEND married (177) LAURA WAY December 31st, 1865.
168. AUGUSTUS TOWNSEND married (178) LIBBIE KEMAN January 1st, 1866
169. CYRUS E. TOWNSEND married (179) EMMA TOWNSEND December 10th, 1865.

---

* "I can not remember all their names."—E. BRIGGS.
† Esther was born October 11th, 1810. They were married April 6th, 1828.

170. ELIZA TOWNSEND married (180) EDWARD WEABER March 25th, 1866.

171. MARTHA TOWNSEND married (181) EDMOND WAY December 29th, 1867.

BENJAMIN TOWNSEND (see page 5)
MARRIED
JOANNA LYON (No. 182).*

They never had any children.

NANCY TOWNSEND (see page 5)
MARRIED
JOHN GILES (No. 183).†

They had eleven children,
184. SUSAN GILES; dead.
185. MARTIN GILES; dead.
186. MAURY GILES; dead.
187. CALISTA GILES; dead.
188. JOHN GILES, Jr., died in Copley, Summit Co., Ohio, September 18th, 1876, aged 80 years.
189. NANCY GILES; dead.
190. ALVIN GILES; dead.
191. —— ——; dead.
192. RYSIA GILES; dead.
193. —— ——; dead.
194. POLLY N. GILES, born July 22d, 1811.

POLLY N. GILES (No. 194)
MARRIED
LORING BRIGGS (No. 195).‡

---

*They were married October 25th, 1792. She was born in Wendall, Mass., March 26th, 1771. They removed to South Stuikeley, Lower Canada, B. N. A., with his youngest brother, Eliphalet, and Hannah Townsend, in the Winter of 1798–99. In the War of 1812–13, Benjamin enlisted in the British service, was soon taken sick, received an honorable discharge, and started for his home, but only lived to reach St. Johns, L. C., where he died June 5th, 1813, aged 44 years and 6 months.

†Nancy died October 7th, 1819, and John died January 16th, 1829, so say John Giles, Jr., of Copley, Ohio, and Huldah (Townsend) St. Clair, of Hampton, Iowa.

‡Loring was born in New Salem, Franklin Co., Mass., May 3d, 1810. They were married in New Salem March 10th, 1832. J. E. Townsend, of Erving, Mass., says they had six grandchildren.

They had six children,

196. DETROIT N. BRIGGS, born in Northfield, Mass., October 4th, 1833; married June 17th, 1863, and died in Erving, Mass., May 27th, 1866.

197. ELLIOT BRIGGS, born in Orange, Mass., April 25th, 1835; died August 27th, 1857.

198. DWIGHT BRIGGS, born in Erving, Mass., August 7th, 1836; married April 11th, 1860.

199. ALBERT BRIGGS, born in Erving, Mass., April 1st, 1838; married December 25th, 1860.

200. MARY BRIGGS, born in Erving, Mass., October 12th, 1842; married December 20th, 1866.

201. JONES L. BRIGGS, born in Erving, Mass., August 29th, 1846; married November 17th, 1869.

POLLY TOWNSEND (see page 5)
MARRIED
DANIEL RICHMOND (No. 202).*

They had three children,

203. BETSEY RICHMOND, born in 1796.
204. SALLY RICHMOND, born in 1798.
205. POLLY RICHMOND, born in 1800.

Widow POLLY TOWNSEND RICHMOND†
MARRIED
Captain RUFUS TYLER (No. 206).

Marriages.

203. BETSEY RICHMOND married (207) DANIEL TIDD, and died in 1853.

204. SALLY RICHMOND married (208) JOSHUA CHAMBERLAIN in 1813. Joshua died January 20th, 1874, aged 82 years, 8 months, and 27 days. "December, 1876, Sally, his widow, lived in the house where her mother died."

205. POLLY RICHMOND married (209) HIRAM TOWN in 1823 or 1824.

---

*They were married in 1795. Daniel died in 1802.

†They were married November, 1813. The Captain died in March, 1816. Great Aunt Polly died in Shrewsbury, Mass., December 27th, 1860, aged 88 years, 6 months, and 10 days. "A true Christian for over sixty years, and for over forty years a member of the M. E. Church. Well beloved by all who knew her."—D. S. C.

ELIPHALET TOWNSEND (see page 5)
MARRIED
HANNAH DAY (No. 210).*

They had twelve children,

211. POLLY TOWNSEND, born in Georgia, Vermont, December 6th, 1798.

212. BETSEY TOWNSEND, born at South Stuikeley, Lower Canada, December 23d, 1800.

213. BENJAMIN TOWNSEND, 2d, born at Stuikeley, L. C., November 15th, 1802.

214. HANNAH TOWNSEND, born at Stuikeley, L. C., May 14th, 1804.

215. ELISHA GREEN TOWNSEND, born at Stuikeley, L. C., January 4th, 1807.

216. PELATIAH DAY TOWNSEND, born at Stuikeley, L. C., August 1st, 1809.

217. HULDAH TOWNSEND, born at Brome, L. C., August 6th, 1813.

218. NANCY TOWNSEND, born at Brome, October 7th, 1815.

219. ABNER TOWNSEND, born at Brome, April 22d, 1817.

220. JONATHAN TOWNSEND, 3d, born at Brome, August 14th, 1820.

221. ELIPHALET TOWNSEND, Jr., born at Brome, July 1st, 1822.

222. ANNA TOWNSEND, born at Brome, September 2d, 1825.

ELIPHALET TOWNSEND, Sr. (second marriage)
MARRIED
ELIZABETH LEWIS (No. 223).†

They had one child,

224. LAURA ADELINE TOWNSEND, born in Brome, L. C., February 16th, 1832.‡

---

* They were married at New Salem, Mass., November 30th, 1797. Hannah was the daughter of Pelatiah Day and Hannah Curtis, and was born January 27th, 1782.

† They were married May 16th, 1831. Elizabeth was born at Shefford, L. C., May 16th, 1796.

‡ All thirteen children lived to be married, all had families except Laura Adeline, who was twice married, but had no children.

NOTE.—About 1809, Eliphalet Townsend paid for one hundred acres of good land in Brome, L. C., on which he lived. He died April 9th, 1850, aged 75 years, 2 months, and 7 days, of the third shock of palsy (or paralysis). It is well said, that he was none the less a man for his having lived fifty-one years in Canada. Hannah, his wife, died at Brome, September 5th, 1829, aged 47 years, 7 months, and 9 days.

POLLY TOWNSEND (No. 211)
MARRIED
WILLIAM TIBBITTS (No. 225).*

They had eight children,

226. PRISCILLA ELLEN TIBBITTS, born September 10th, 1820.
227. WILLIAM WALLACE, born October 19th, 1822.
228. NAAMAN URIAH, born January 30th, 1825.
229. URSULA DELIA, born December 1st, 1826.
230. ELIPHALET J., born February 18th, 1829; died January, 1830.
231. TOWNSEND E., born March 18th, 1832.
232. ELISHA B.
233. LEEMAN.

BETSEY TOWNSEND (No. 212)†
MARRIED
GEORGE C. TIBBITTS (No. 234).

They had five children,
235. SAMANTHA.
236. NELSON B.
237. ALONZO.
238. ROSETTA.
239. HANNAH A.

Elder BENJAMIN TOWNSEND (No. 213)
MARRIED
ESTHER HALE (No. 240).‡

They had four children,

241. BENJAMIN DELTA TOWNSEND, born at Orange, Franklin Co., Mass., July 9th, 1825.
242. ABNER P. TOWNSEND, born at Orange, Mass., April 7th, 1827.

---

*They were married about 1818 or 1819. William was born February 11th, 1795. Polly died in 1873.

† Betsey died at Westminister, Upper Canada, July 16th, 1847.

‡ They were married August 26th, 1824. Benjamin died at Northfield South Farms, Mass., November 22d, 1831, aged 29 years and 7 days. Esther was born at Petersham, Mass., January 22d, 1795, and died at Winchester, Cheshire Co., N. H., June 23d, 1862, aged 67 years, 5 months, and 1 day.

243. SAMUEL DAY TOWNSEND, born at Ervings Grant (now South Orange), Franklin Co., Mass., July 9th, 1829.

244. JOHN ELIPHALET TOWNSEND, born at Northfield South Farms, Franklin Co., Mass., July 9th, 1831.

HANNAH TOWNSEND (No. 214)
MARRIED
JOHN WESLEY WHITEHEAD (No. 245).*

They had ten children,

246. SAMANTHA MELISSA, born December 26th, 1825.
247. JOHN WESLEY, Jr., born January 27th, 1828; died June 11th, 1828.
248. HANNAH TOWNSEND, born September 24th, 1829.
249. NANCY MELINDA, born December 16th, 1831.
250. ELIPHALET MYRON, born March 16th, 1835.
251. JONATHAN WESLEY, born September 20th, 1837.
252. AARON PELATIAH, born September 5th, 1840.
253. LAURA ANNA, born June 22d, 1843.
254. DAVID BENJAMIN, born October 1st, 1846; died December 4th, 1850.
255. WILLIAM, 2d, born March 25th, 1849.

ELISHA GREEN TOWNSEND (No. 215)†
MARRIED
ARVILLA BALL (No. 256).

They had one child,

257. LINDSEY DAY TOWNSEND, born at Brome, L. C., August 26th, 1833.

PELATIAH DAY TOWNSEND (No. 216)
MARRIED
ELIZA W. CUTTING (No. 258).‡

---

*They were married March 13th, 1825. John was born at Fairfield, Vt., March 6th, 1801.

†They were married January 27th, 1833. Arvilla was born at Brome, L. C., August 24th, 1813. Elisha died at Brome December 13th, 1835, after suffering three days from being badly frozen, while returning home from Frost Village, five miles distant. He had succeeded in arriving at the west end of the bridge over Brome Lake, one mile from his home, when he fell, and lay eight or ten hours before he was found.

‡They were married October 4th, 1842. Eliza was born August 31st, 1821. Pelatiah died at Lebanon, N. H., July 5th, 1872.

They had one child,

259. RALPH CUTTING TOWNSEND, born October 27th, 1843.

HULDAH TOWNSEND (No. 217)

MARRIED

ORRIN HACKSTAFF (No. 260).*

They had seven children,

261. MARY ELIZABETH ANNA MARIAH HACKSTAFF, born at New Lebanon, N. Y., September 11th, 1839.

262. ISADORA ANTINET, born June 8th, 1842; died October 9th, 1855.

263. ELLEN SOPHI, born May 5th, 1845.

264. ALICE EFFI, born August 27th, 1846.

265. CHARLOTTE LORANE, born November 20th, 1848; died at Holyoke, Mass., June 14th, 1867.

266. ROSETTA SALLY, born December 22d, 1850; died December 15th, 1853.

267. EMMA NANCY, born December 7th, 1852.

NANCY TOWNSEND (No. 218)

MARRIED

HENRY LAWRENCE, Jr. (No. 268).†

They had eight children,

269. HANNAH ELIZABETH, born January 17th, 1839; died December 12th, 1854, of consumption.

270. DORCAS, born December 25th, 1840; died June 21st, 1841.

271. NATHAN PARKER, born August 24th, 1842.

272. SIMON ELISHA, born August 2d, 1845; died May 13th, 1865.

273. GUILFORD DUDLEY, born October 7th, 1847.

274. AZARIAH WELCOME, born September 22d, 1851.

275. ADELINE, born December 7th, 1855.

276. URI TOWNSEND, born August 17th, 1859.

---

*They were married in 1839. Orrin was born at Virgennes, Vt., March 24th, 1801, and died at Lowell, Vt., July 13th, 1860. He was a miller by trade. He was a Universalist.

†They were married April 9th, 1838. Henry was born at Lawrenceville, L. C., November 6th, 1817, and died in his own house at Lawrenceville, May 20th, 1871. His trade was that of a house builder. He was a Methodist.

ABNER TOWNSEND (No. 219)
MARRIED
LUCY COOK (No. 277).*

They had four children,
278. EMARY ALLEN, born February 16th, 1844.
279. WILLIAM COOK, born March 7th, 1846.
280. POLLY T., born January 25th, 1848.
281. RACHEL LORAIN, born January 21st, 1855. All four were born at Brome, L. C., B. N. A., and removed to Lyme Centre, N. H., in 1865.

JONATHAN TOWNSEND, 3D. (No. 220)
MARRIED
ELIZABETH FRENCH (No. 282).†

They had seven children,
283. GEORGE RILEY, born August 17th, 1841.
284. ANNA TYRESSA, born April 20th, 1843; died May 3d, 1843.
285. MARY ADELINE, born March 19th, 1844.
286. HARRISON ELWIN, born March 24th, 1846; died January 28th, 1847.
287. HARRISON ARTHUR, born November 20th, 1847. He enlisted in the army in the Fall of 1863, was captured by the rebels in September, 1864, and died in Salisbury prison, North Carolina, November 29th, 1864.
288. ISADORA MELISSA, born June 1st, 1849.
289. CELIA ANNETTIE, born August 28th, 1851.

ELIPHALET TOWNSEND JR. (No. 221)
MARRIED
ANN MARIAH GEORGE (No. 290).‡

They had six children,
291. AMANDA MARIAH, born December 15th, 1844.

---

* Lucy was of Corinth, Vt., and they were married October 23d, 1842. She was born September 6th, 1817. Abner died at Lyme Centre, N. H., June 2d, 1876. He was a Freewill Baptist, and by trade a farmer.

† They were married November 9th, 1840. Elizabeth was born at Stuikeley, L. C., March 23d, 1820.

‡ They were married February 5th, 1844. Ann Mariah was born at Stoneham, Mass., February 3d, 1826. Eliphalet, Jr., died at his father's residence in Brome, L. C., March 18th, 1859, of lung and liver consumption, aged 36 years, 8 months, and 17 years.

292. MARY ROSETTA, born July 23d, 1848; died September 12th, 1849.
293. MARTHA ROSETTA, born July 29th, 1850; died November 10th, 1851.
294. EMMY ROZILLA, born December 10th, 1852.
295. JONATHAN ELIPHALET, born April 20th, 1855; died October 9th, 1855.
296. MALCOM ELIPHALET, born October 8th, 1856.

Marriages of Eliphalet and Ann Mariah Townsend's Children.

291. AMANDA M. TOWNSEND married (297) GEORGE H. PERKINS, of Bolton, L. C., November 1st, 1869.
294. EMMY ROZILLA TOWNSEND married (298) MIRUM COONS, of Bolton, L. C., November 1st, 1869.

ANNA TOWNSEND (No. 222)

MARRIED

SILAS JACKMAN COOK (No. 299).*

They had three children,
300. EDWARD BENJAMIN, born April 2d, 1845.
301. WILLIAM ALLEN, born June 7th, 1846; and was instantly killed by a Southern rebel's bullet, while in active battle, fighting for the Federal Government of the U. S. A., May 5th, 1864.
302. ACHSAH, born January 25th, 1848.

LAURA ADELINE TOWNSEND (No. 224)

MARRIED

STEWARD LEWIS (No. 303).†

---

*They were married January 1st, 1844. Silas was born at Corinth, Vt., June 15th, 1815, and died January 20th, 1848. He was a Freewill Baptist, and by trade a farmer. Anna, his wife, died at her father's residence, July 2d, 1855.

† They were married about January, 1850, and after spending all of Laura's property, he forsook her while she was dangerously sick with a fever, at Rutland, Vt., December 31st, 1851, and fled to Canada. After a time Laura recovered, and the people at Rutland helped her with money to return to her mother's. In 1854 and 1855 Laura resided at Barton, Vt., near to where Steward took another woman, driving him home to Lower Canada, while she procured a decree of divorce from him.

NOTE.—Hannah Townsend, Eliphalet, Sr., Eliphalet, Jr., Anna, and three of the children of Eliphalet Townsend, Jr. and Ann M. George, his wife. were all buried on the farm of Eliphalet Townsend, Sr., in Brome, L. C., on a rise of land north of the house.

LAURA ADELINE TOWNSEND (second marriage)
MARRIED
FILANDER SARTLE (No. 304).*

Fourth Generation—Jonathan, Sr., Eliphalet, Sr., Benjamin, 2d.
BENJAMIN DELTA TOWNSEND (No. 241)
MARRIED
NANCY M. WHITEHEAD (No. 249).†

They had six children,

305. LOIS, born at Wolcott, Vt., August 19th, 1850.

306. AMI, born at Brome, L. C., July 27th, 1852; died in West Swanzey, N. H., March 11th, 1855.

307. VASHTI VICTORIA, born at West Swanzey, N. H., June 27th, 1855.

308. NAOMI DEBORAH, born at Brome, L. C., February 21st, 1857; died July 16th, 1863.

309. ZILLAH TABOR, born at Richford, Vt., October 14th, 1859.

310. MIRIAM MAACHAH, born at Richford, Vt., November 3d, 1861.

ABNER P. TOWNSEND (No. 242)
MARRIED
LYDIA HALE (No. 311).‡

They had two children,

312. EMILY JANE, born at Richmond, N. H., March 11th, 1847.

313. ELLA J., born at Winchester, N. H., October 17th, 1848.

EMILY J. TOWNSEND (No. 312)
MARRIED
FRANK B. WRIGHT (No. 314).§

---

*Soon after their marriage, in the Spring of 1856, they removed from Barton, Vt., to Laura's mother's, at Lawrenceville, L. C., where Mr. Sartle purchased a farm near the village. Laura died at her home May 9th, 1857, not delivered.

† They were married at Dunham, L. C., July 9th, 1849, by Rev. Nelson Kimball, an English Wesleyan Methodist minister, and removed to the United States in 1850. She was from Brome.

‡ They were married at Vernon, Vt., June 25th, 1846, by Washburn, Esq. Lydia was born at Richmond, N. H., September 30th, 1826.

§ They were married in Orange, Franklin Co., Mass., May, 1870.

ELLA J. TOWNSEND (No. 313)
MARRIED
FRANK E. FOSTER (No. 315).*

They had one child,

316. CHARLES EDWARD FOSTER, born at Athol, Mass., March 20th, 1874.

SAMUEL DAY TOWNSEND (No. 243)
MARRIED
LOVISA FRENCH (No. 317).†

They had six children,

318. AMARIAH HOMER, born September 1st, 1849; died in Brome, L. C., October 29th, 1850.

319. MARTHA ELIZABETH, born April 20th, 1851; died at Delaware, Delaware Co., Iowa, September 11th, 1871.

320. AARON, born December 18th, 1853.

321. ALVIN, born April 3d, 1855.

322. LAURA ESTHER, born February 10th, 1861; died at Wayne, Jones Co., Iowa, February 1st, 1863.

323. VICTOR HUGO ALBERT TOWNSEND, born at Delaware, Delaware Co., Iowa, April 9th, 1869.

AARON TOWNSEND (No. 320)
MARRIED
JULIA BERGES (No. 324).

[They were married November 4th, 1876.]

JOHN ELIPHALET TOWNSEND (No. 244)
MARRIED
NANCY JANE THAYER (No. 325).‡

They had no children.

---

* They were married October 17th, 1870. He was born July 27th, 1850.

† They were married in Brome, L. C., November 22d, 1848. She was born in Brome, July 7th, 1830.

‡ They were married at Petersham, Mass., February 24th, 1853. Nancy was born at Athol, Mass., December 10th, 1831, and died in West Dummerston, Vt., November 5th, 1876.

JOHN E. TOWNSEND (second marriage)
MARRIED
Mrs. LUCY ANNA MILLER (No. 326).*

They had one child,

327. JOHN EDWARD TOWNSEND, born at West Brattleboro, Vt., March 21st, 1879.

RALPH CUTTING TOWNSEND (No. 259)
MARRIED
CYNTHIA HASTINGS (No. 328).†

They had two children,

329. ELIZABETH C. TOWNSEND, born at Lebanon, N. H., March 6th, 1873.

330. AUGUSTUS ABIGAIL TOWNSEND, born at Lebanon, June 7th, 1875.

MARY E. A. M. HACKSTAFF (No. 261)
MARRIED
LEWIS SHUFELT (No. 331).‡

They had three children,

332. JULIA ESTELLA SHUFELT, born July 24th, 1862.
333. MARY ELLEN SHUFELT, born January 2d, 1866.
334. HADEN MORRIS SHUFELT, born July 23d, 1869.

NELLE SOPHI HACKSTAFF (No. 263)
MARRIED
CHARLES W. ROBERTSON (No. 335).§

They had two children,

336. NELLIE ADELLE ROBERTSON, born December 28th, 1874.

337. CHARLES ARBA ROBERTSON, born November 11th, 1877.

---

* They were married at Brattleboro, Vt., January 3d, 1878. He was from Erving, Mass., and she from West Brattleboro. Lucy was the daughter of Calvin Gould, and was born at Chicopee, Mass., November 25th, 1839.

† They were married December 24th, 1863.

‡ They were married July 4th, 1861.

§ They were married August 30th, 1870.

ALICE EFFI HACKSTAFF (No. 264)
MARRIED
OSCAR CUTTING (No. 338).*

They had three children,

339. ARTHUR BYRON CUTTING, born October 19th, 1873; died July 2d, 1874.
340. LOTTIE D. CUTTING, born March 15th, 1875.
341. EUGENE WILFRED CUTTING, born June 27th, 1878. Residence, Lyme Centre, N. H.

EMMA NANCY HACKSTAFF (No. 267)
MARRIED
ARBA NELSON (No. 342).†

They had no children.

NATHAN PARKER LAWRENCE (No. 271)
MARRIED
Mrs. MELINDA M. J. GREGORY (No. 343).‡

They had one child,

344. Son, born June 4th, 1876; died June 4th, 1876.

AZARIAH WELCOME LAWRENCE (No. 274)
MARRIED
EMMA RANDALL (No. 345).§

They had one child,

346. HENRY WELLINGTON ALLEN LAWRENCE, born at Lawrenceville, L. C., March 23d, 1878.

EMARY ALLEN TOWNSEND (No. 278)
MARRIED
CLARA L. HOYT (No. 347).||

---

* They were married January 1st, 1873. Oscar was born August 6th, 1847.
† They were married September 1st, 1876. He was from Craftsbury, Vt.
‡ They were married at Ebensburg, Columbia Co., Pa., March 23d, 1875.
§ They were married December 2d, 1876.
|| She was from Newport, Orleans Co., Vt. They were married March 3d, 1870. Clara was born January 26th, 1850.

They had three children,

348. CARRIE BELL TOWNSEND, born in Newport, Vt., March 17th, 1872.
349. NETTIE AMIE TOWNSEND, born in Essex, Vt., December 21st, 1873.
350. WILLIAM ABNER TOWNSEND, born in Newport, Vt., November 26th, 1876.

WILLIAM COOK TOWNSEND (No. 279)
MARRIED
MARY A. LAWRENCE (No. 351).*

They had no children.

GEORGE RILEY TOWNSEND (No. 283)
MARRIED
FRANCELIA D. OBER (No. 352).†

They had five children,

353. ARTHUR HARRISON, born February 24th, 1867.
354. GRACE RUDELL, born November 28th, 1868.
355. LIZZIE ONETTIE, born October 20th, 1869.
356. MYRTLE IVY, born December 22d, 1874.
357. MAUD EVERLY, born May 6th, 1878.

MARY ADELINE TOWNSEND (No. 285)
MARRIED
ALBERT J. COOK (No. 358).‡

They had one child,

359. ARTHUR EDWARD COOK, born April 5th, 1866.

ISADORA MELISSA TOWNSEND (No. 288)
MARRIED
FRANKLIN B. ATWELL (No. 360).§

---

* Mary was from Lawrenceville, L. C. They were married October 9th, 1867. She was born October 6th, 1847.

† They were married at Johnson, Lamoille Co., Vt., April 26th, 1866.

‡ They were married in Johnson, Vt., December 28th, 1864. Albert died May 21st, 1867.

§ They were married in Johnson, Vt., April 26th, 1866.

They had four children,

361. ALICE ELIZABETH ATWELL, born May 15th, 1869; died November 28th, 1877.
362. FRANKLIN EDWARD ATWELL, born December 14th, 1872; died May 19th, 1874.
363. ELDORA EVERLY ATWELL, born April 24th, 1875.
364. ETTA MAY ATWELL, born March 10th, 1877.

CELIA ANNETTIE TOWNSEND (No. 289)
MARRIED
DANN. D. SMITH (No. 365).*

They had no children.

Gilbert W. Townsend's Family Record—Continued from Page 15.

Chester (172) and Mary Townsend Plummer (161) had four children:

366. HENRY M. PLUMMER, born November 30th, 1850.
367. ARTHUR PLUMMER, born November 7th, 1852; died December 16th, 1863.
368. MARY E. PLUMMER, born March 23d, 1855.
369. IDA PLUMMER, born June 1st, 1858; died September 15th, 1874.

HENRY M. PLUMMER (No. 366)
MARRIED
LOVINA KERNAN (No. 370).†

They had one child,
371. CHESTER M. PLUMMER, born May 7th, 1877.

MARY E. PLUMMER (No. 368)
MARRIED
CHARLES E. PHILLIPS (No. 372).‡

Mrs. Dulcenia Townsend Duel (162) died January 1st, 1859, leaving no children.

---

* They were married at Cambridge, Lamoille Co., Vt., June 29th, 1875.

† They were married January 7th, 1874. Lovina was born July 13th, 1850.

‡ They were married December 23d, 1874. Charles was born February 11th, 1850, and died April 23d, 1875.

GENEALOGY OF JONATHAN TOWNSEND.

Albert U. (163) and Elizabeth Townsend (174) had two children:

373. ASA TOWNSEND, born December 15th, 1854.
374. JOSEPHENE TOWNSEND, born December 28th, 1858.

Charles D. (166) and Lazellee Townsend (176) had one child:

375. LEWIS TOWNSEND, born May 5th, 1861.

Augustus (168) and Libbie Townsend (178) had two children:

376. LYSANDER G. TOWNSEND, born November 26th, 1867.
377. MELVIN TOWNSEND, born January 28th, 1872.

Cyrus E. (169) and Emma Townsend (179) had two children:

378. WILLIE TOWNSEND, born September 2d, 1868.
379. HATTIE TOWNSEND, born January 11th, 1872.

Eliza Townsend (170) and Edward Weaber (180) had four children:

380. GILBERT B. WEABER, born December 15th, 1867.
381. ARTHUR P. WEABER, born April 6th, 1868.
382. ESSIE T. WEABER, born August 21st, 1870.
383. CLARA WEABER, born June 20th, 1872.

Sally Richmond (204) and Joshua Chamberlain (208) had five children living in 1875:

384. POLLY CHAMBERLAIN married (385) JASPER BASSET, and lived in Tarnumville (Grafton).
386. DANIEL STETSON CHAMBERLAIN, lived in Shrewsbury, Mass.
387. SARAH CHAMBERLAIN married (388) —— HOLBROOK, and lived in Shrewsbury with her mother.
389. NANCY CHAMBERLAIN, born in South Orange, Mass., November 5th, 1821, married (390) ETHAN BULLARD.*
391. JOSHUA CHAMBERLAIN married, and lived in Oakdale (West Boylston) Mass.

Nancy (389) and Ethan Bullard (390) had nine children:

392. MARTIN BULLARD, born in Westborough, Mass., February 19th, 1844, carpenter, married (393) LIBBIE MOWER, in North Brookfield, Mass., May 9th, 1867.

---

* Ethan was the son of Martin and Nabby (Corey) Bullard, and was born in Westborough, Mass., August 11th, 1816. His occupation is that of carpenter, joiner, and stair builder. He married Nancy Chamberlain in Shrewsbury, Mass., September 1st, 1840, and settled in Westborough, where they lived till January 1st, 1865, when they moved to Dundee, Ill.; remaining there till June 1st, 1865, when they removed to Elgin, Ill., where they now reside.

394. MARY AUGUSTA BULLARD, born in Westborough, August 14th, 1847; died August 29th, 1847.

395. MARTHA BULLARD, born in Westborough, July 9th, 1849; died November 7th, 1849.

396. JANE MARIA BULLARD, born in Westborough, October 20th, 1850, married May 25th, 1869, (397) WICKLIFF S. LONG, of Elgin, Ill., where they now reside. He is a painter and grainer.

398. LUCY ANN BULLARD, born in Westborough, September 8th, 1852; died December 22d, 1855.

399. GEORGE BULLARD, born in Westborough, December 14th, 1853, stone cutter, married, December 14th, 1875, (400) ANN HICKEY, of South Elgin, Ill., and resides in Elgin.

401. CHARLES BULLARD, born in Westborough, August 17th, 1855; died October 3d, 1855.

402. WILLIE BULLARD, born February 9th, 1857; died May 5th, 1858.

403. JOHN TYLER BULLARD, born February 15th, 1859.

NOTE.—Up to present date, I have given all the births, marriages, and deaths of all our kindred from whom I have received their record, and of all the Townsend women to their third generation. For some unknown cause, three families have not reported, to whom I had sent duplicate letters one year ago, with stamps in all.   COMPILER.

LIME SPRING, Iowa, April 14th, 1879.

HISTORY.

Eliphalet Townsend, Sr., the son of Jonathan and Huldah Townsend, of New Salem, Franklin Co., Mass., left his native home in the Spring of 1796, to seek a home in what was at that time the wild woods of Lower Canada. Arriving at East Farnham, L. C., Eliphalet fell in with a man who said that he had the title to some land in East Farnham. After Eliphalet made his selection, he paid $100 for one hundred acres of land, receiving what he really believed to be a true title; and, with a pioneer's will, he began to clear up a farm for himself.

In 1849, I hired out to a young man by the name of Wells, for one month, in haying. One day the old gentleman, Wells, came with a jug of water and a lunch for me. While I was eating, he said, "Then you are grandson of Eliphalet Townsend, are you?" I said, yes. Then he said, "The land where you have been mowing to-day is the land that Eliphalet Townsend really supposed he had a true title of in 1796; but my father and his family had twelve hundred acres of wild land granted us on condition that we should permanently settle in Lower Canada. After we had settled, on surveying most of our land, we came to the corner of this lot, and, hearing the sound of an ax, we came here and found quite a clearing made. We told Eliphalet that we were the lawful owners of this very lot. He disputed our claim, and produced his paper. We had heard of the man who was deeding false titles, and told Eliphalet so. We all went to the Crown Records, and proved our title to this very lot. And as we learned that the man who sold Eliphalet the land had fled the country, we gave him a small sum for his betterments, and he left."

Eliphalet says, "After losing my land and money, I returned to New Salem, Mass., worked out, and in due time was married. After a while, we removed to Georgia, Vermont, and, after the birth of Polly, we came into Canada with my brother Benjamin, and Joanna his wife, about February, 1799. Benjamin went to the Crown Records, proved his title, and paid for one hundred acres of land in South Stuikeley, and made himself a home. But as I had no money, I squatted, cleared up a farm, sold my betterments at a fair price, and then bought this farm in Brome, two miles from Frost Village in Shefford, and two miles from Jones's Mills on the outlet of Brome Lake, and were it not for the big doctor's bills that I have paid, I should now be a rich man."

All agree that Eliphalet Townsend became a true professor of religion when about fifty years of age. He always disapproved of war, and only enlisted in the British service to prevent being mobbed. After marching to St. Johns he was honorably discharged, as peace had just been declared. Eliphalet became a firm believer in the religion of the Friends, and died such.

Benjamin Townsend, 2d, son of Eliphalet Townsend, Sr., became a pillar in society and in the church. At an early day he became as true a Christian as ever joined the Methodist Episcopal Church. At about twenty-one years of age he was ordained a local preacher, and continued to preach as long as his health would admit. From 1828 to 1831, the church and conference besought him to take a circuit, and be ordained a circuit preacher, but his faith in the life of St. Paul, "to first provide for his family, and then preach the gospel free," was the means that caused him to lie down and die young. As an honest husband and father, as an honest Christian and neighbor, none have ever excelled Elder Benjamin Townsend. Had he been blessed with a college education, with the Heaven-born talent that he possessed, and had he given his whole time to the church, none would have ever been found better fitted for a minister's life than he. His error consisted in accepting Paul's life in preference to the commands of Jesus Christ in Matthew 28: 19, 20. He was not long sick, a cold in his head ending in his death in about two weeks. Many have mourned his early departure. As a man with only a common school education, his Creator did not see fit to let him suffer long for his error in faith.

From his history, we turn to his brother, Pelatiah Day Townsend, a man less favored with an education, who for years has been afflicted with dimness of eyes, and who for a year was entirely blind. He had not recovered good eye sight when he was married. As a lay member in the Freewill Baptist Church, it may well be said that he was one of her strong pillars. Notwithstanding his earthly troubles, Pelatiah was a consistent Christian, and one who was for a number of years of much help to the little church where he lived. His voice in prayer or in speaking was such as most generally to command the attention of all in the meeting, whether they were professors of religion or not. To get acquainted with Pelatiah D. Townsend was to get acquainted with an honest man. He is missed both in the church and out of the church. Scrofula slowly but surely brought him to the grave. He was a good farmer, and respected wherever known.

Their youngest brother, Eliphalet Townsend, Jr., excepting in solemn appearance, was more like his brother Benjamin, a deep thinker, and one who held fast to the truth that he accepted. Being a Freewill Baptist, he was not so often in the pulpit as was his brother Benjamin, but his daily life was a continual sermon. The two years that I was acquainted with him, I can not remember ever seeing him laugh. I have no doubt but he was aware that he must meet an early death. He died of lung and liver consumption.

I have not singled out these men as being better than the Townsends in general; no, but having no other history, and knowing these men, I could not do otherwise than tell a little of what I really did know, meaning no offense to any one.

CORRECTIONS.

On page 15, foot note (*), page 17, and wherever else it may occur, read Stukely, instead of Stuikeley.

On page 20, No. 275, read Adaline Lorinda.

On page 20, foot note (†), read "Henry was born at South Stukely, L. C.," instead of at Lawrenceville.

On page 25, No. 263, read "Ellen Sophi," instead of Nelle; see page 20, No. 263.

The above mistakes are cheerfully corrected. There may be others; however, we have failed to see them, taking letters and manuscripts for our guide.

Milton Keynes UK
Ingram Content Group UK Ltd.
UKHW021950251023
431347UK00005B/46